the book of
jade

apryl yvonne scott

The Book of Jade

Copyright © 2021 Apryl Yvonne Scott.

Produced and printed by Stillwater River Publications.

Visit our website at **www.StillwaterPress.com** for more information.

First Stillwater River Publications Edition

ISBN: 978-1-952521-09-6

1 2 3 4 5 6 7 8 9 10
Written by Apryl Yvonne Scott
Published by Stillwater River Publications
Pawtucket, RI, USA.

Publisher's Cataloging-In-Publication Data
(Prepared by The Donohue Group, Inc.)

Names: Scott, Apryl Yvonne, author.
Title: The book of jade / Apryl Yvonne Scott.
Description: First Stillwater River Publications edition. |
Pawtucket, RI, USA : Stillwater River Publications, [2021]
Identifiers: ISBN 9781952521096
Subjects: LCSH: Scott, Apryl Yvonne--Poetry.
| LCGFT: Poetry.
Classification: LCC PS3619.C652 B66 2020 |
DDC 813/.6--dc23

acknowledgements

With sincere and earnest love, respect, and gratitude.
To my family and friends, thank you.

an introduction

This is me, putting into words my
Pursuit of happiness. Though
Everything that gleams, isn't
Always gold, I know I'll find my way.
I'm good. I'm determined to get there.

—Ophelia

poetry in reflection

It's amazing how different our words can be, miraculous how clear the picture becomes, when the awakening begins. Here, I have unearthed myself. And now bask relentlessly in my love of words. I have always loved words, the way they sound, how they seem to shift and move, how different arrangements whisk you away to unusual places, moments, feelings, time. Clear articulation of who I am and who I thought I was supposed to be never came with ease. Manifestation of my hopes, dreams, and aspirations were but a mere mirage. In writing, I discovered a way to bring to life these many parts of myself, scrabbling to breathe, beseeching to be set free. Unrestricted, they dance, they sing, they assemble, they inspire. With a heart blessed by Midas, I reach out to the world. And may everything turn to Gold.

SI·DE·RE·AL

sī'dirēəl/

adjective

: of or with respect to the distant stars*

stay awake

S Sidereal, alabaster night;
T Translucent, alabaster sight;
A An arcane, method of flight;
Y Yore images return me to high heights.

A Amethyst shadows, shake me with fright, but
W Wake, I shall not;
A Along this nightly ride; for in this moment,
K Providence remains my guide, on this;
E Everlasting alabaster night.

baby girl

Baby girl please stop your crying.
I can't bear to see you cry.
Soon the world will know,
How lovely you are inside.
Few will take the time to admire,
The wonders you may do.
Try to remember the ones who matter,
Are the ones who appreciate you.

painting dreams

It burns,
And from the ashes it grows.
This classic tale of friend and foe.
Good against evil, the lengthiest of tales,
High and mighty, does the shadow sphere dwell.
Carrying out its mission, its purpose to tell.

Barring the mark,
Such a burden to bear.
Scorched, branded,
Sullied by solar flare.
Leering at gentle violent,
Unyielding and light.

Safe from evil,
Far from harm,
Lingering behind as if,
There were no cause,
for alarm.

flatu fluta

F   Frequent sounds and syllables,
L   Lain in intricate intervals,
A   Augment the situation, critical,
T   Transfigure the moment, literal,
U   Utopia drifts vaguely near.
F   Fragile feelings transpire,
L   Legato, lain, asunder,
U   Ubiquitous, pleasure,
T   Cohering to this fixture,
A   Abstruse, no longer, mine eyes, see clear.

note to self

Hello Marcus,

I wish I were my chipper self today, but alas I am not. The day has continued to weigh heavy on my chest, and I fear I will not be able to fend off these demons before nightfall. To shake this trepidation indefinitely; what a splendid thought. Perhaps, I derive my vigor from my fear of failure. If only my desire might exact my greatest ambitions, then...I could be free.

Always with joy in my heart,
Ophelia

he lives

His words, they triggered something,
And visions arrived;
Akin to freshly printed pages off a printing press.
My regards to this particular man born a poet, and
May I too become like the rose he so warmly spoke of;
The Rose That Grew From Concrete.

PO·ET·RY

ˈpōətrē

noun

: literary work in which special attention and intensity
is given to distinctive style and rhythm

: a characterized quality of beauty
and intensity of emotion

: the art of rhythmical composition,
written or spoken, for exciting pleasure
by beautiful, imaginative, or
elevated thoughts

scream

I scream,

But, there is, no sound.

No air, in either direction to be found.

Beating hard in my chest.

My head churns round.

Without rest.

Exhausted.

I recoil.

in a hurry

I always feel
I am being followed;
Though there is never anyone trailing.
I stop to think.
But never mind.
Just random thoughts.
Casual, anonymous, gone.

An empty slate sits where once sat,
An absolute certainty.
For a moment, I knew.
For just a moment;
I thought I knew.

To be patient.
That Time,
Is an Enormity;
you can never Hurry.

unbearable

I've just about given up on relationships;
But still, I believe in true love.
However, the notion of never finding it,
Is unbearable.

smitten

Smitten am I.
Not in love But, I am
Dazzled, by how brilliantly he shone.
Images blur, eyes reel back, then
I smile, a brilliant smile.
And my heart begins to sing,
Because my lips have no words.

insatiable

Miss: I miss you already…

Sir: Insatiable urge to kiss you… everywhere

Sir: Was that too much?

Miss: Not at all Sir, we just have different ways
 of saying the same thing…

Sir: Insatiable.

current events

These,
current events.
That was one of the last conversations I had,
Was about current events.

The events of the day, Oh my!
I cannot convey,
my distaste for this confusion.
These current events;
Like heat through hot grates, I vent;
These current events.

Shock me, sway me,
Cause me to display behavior unbecoming of a lady;
Such as myself.

These current events,
Leave a foul stench;
One that cannot be stifled.

It is, irrefutable.

These current events,
these ordeals.
Occasionally in life,
shit is just unbelievably,
Unreal.

witty kisses

I haven't it in me to be coy this evening,
For sake of pleasantry or pride.
I haven't stopped thinking about you.
I am thinking of you now;
And will be thinking of you later.
You've ensnared me with your witty kisses,
And I want more… so many more.

JAD·ED

ˈjādəd/

adjective

: made dull, apathetic, or cynical by experience
or by disappointment

: the end result of having a steady flow of negative
experiences, disappointments, and fulfillment fed
into a person until they come to a point of emotional
arrest and succumb to disillusionment

: an individual who has experienced more energy
than he or she is spiritually allotted and is left feeling
empty, disheartened, disenchanted, jaded

hard like diamonds

The beginning was hard,
Atlas tricks on my shoulders,
Gravity compressing me,
Small.
Till I shine,
Like
Diamonds.

god, fire

I don't mean to overstep any boundaries…
But I can't help that you excite me.
God.

Like the fire from a thousand Suns.
You ignite me.

You stimulate me, not only
Physically, but mentally, spiritually.
And yes, it drives me crazy.

Because I know, that I am only experiencing a fraction
of the magnitude,
That is you.

i apologized

I apologized, for asking questions, I didn't want to ask,
For inquiring about things, I knew, you didn't
    want to discuss,
And for having only the assumptions you have left
    me with.

I said I was sorry,
because I was praying that I was wrong,
that I had indirectly accused you
of something untrue,

For looking into your eyes,
And not being able to communicate this then,
For fear of what it could mean,
I was sorry.

what it is

It's the sultry sound of your voice.
The sullen expressions on your face.
Your, unexpected tenderness.

It seems neither of us have been looking, but

I believe,
I've stumbled upon something.
Rather, someone special.

I look forward to the jolt I feel
when in anticipation of your touch,

My heart races,
My soul ascends,
Time quickens up close, and
slows all around.

I respect how you feel, but
That hasn't altered the way I feel.

Perhaps it should.
Perhaps I'm being foolish.

Or perhaps,
I simply fail to see the fault,
in possibly causing you to smile.

harrowing

I find myself harrowing;
somewhere between lust and formality,
as you occupy spaces in my mind
that would cause even the most
experienced temptress to blush.

dearest

Dearest,
I desire you, immensely.
Please,
Devour me,
Mercilessly.
Till I am overcome with exhaustion.
Sincerely,
submissive

all of me

All of me is flooded with emotion at the thought of you,
And I am forced to reshape my composure
Time,
and time again,
Till you draw near,
And I am able,
to let go.

something nice

I may blush every time you have something nice to say,
 but honestly, it's nice to hear;
not because I like the attention,
but because I believe you are being sincere.

RE·FLEC·TION

rə'flekSH(ə)n/

noun

: a thought, idea, or opinion formed or remarked
as a result of meditation

: an often obscure or indirect inquiry of the mind

: consideration of some subject matter,
hypothesis, or purpose

far away

I would wait for you.
I know because
I've been waiting for you.
I've wished for you
To be waiting for me.
But you couldn't be real.
Dreams, are not real.
And yet, here you are.

Through time for you.
This life and all others for you.
Once upon a time
I Died for you.
In that moment, my heart skipped.
And my spirit rose.
Filching my breath away.

Time lapses,
while latent in your eyes,
Delivering me
far away.

desist

I am slightly disquieted by my intense longing;
An irresistible urge
To send and respond to messages.
Then a swell of resentment
Deafens my senses.
Nay, I say.
This time,
I will resist.

fading

Fading,
in and out of consciousness, I realized;
my attempts to become less of a distraction have
backfired terribly.
My actions,
or lack thereof, for that matter,
may have allowed you to focus,
but I have failed at allotting myself the same courtesy.

a dreamer lost

I too had a dream;
A dream so grand;
A dreamer lost;
Could not withstand;
So great was this dream;
One shed a tear;
For the dream,
a dreamer lost.

many dreams

I've had many dreams,
That one day
I'd wake up
And the world
Would be grander
Than it was the morning before.

magnificent cunt

A Man once said to a Woman,
"You're a magnificent cunt."
And the Woman humbly replied,
"Thank you."

fin.

know thy self

Passion Ambition Beauty, three gifts of the mind that drive me, to fear nothing, give nothing, and perceive all things through a third eye.

With every day that goes by, Passion Ambition Beauty, enhance truly, the sensations these words create.

They build me up then break me down. I'll break it down, Passion Ambition Beauty, have found a way to connect, destroy, and bisect, the whys of the wonders which cause us to wander, amidst the thunder and beyond the rain, across unsound terrain to attain anything of no significance.

With every meander, I feed on what may cling to me, the Caged Bird Sings to me and its song harmoniously lullabies me to rest, with the knowledge that I am, one of the best. Many a time before had I passed that test of self-discovery. Now, in my mind, my world, none is above me. This is my reality. My interpretation of what is and lies beneath thee.

For this, I could never be sorry.

Sincerely,
Passion Ambition Beauty

professor troglodyte

My first semester of college I was warned by English professor who told me my writing might be overly wordy for my audiences. During our first peer review, he blatantly made obvious to the class that he was in accordance with their criticisms. According to the hoard, I was making use of too many BIG words in my writing. The fact that the word BIG was chosen to describe the many words the class failed to comprehend spoke volumes. I am not a fan of dumbing myself down for the masses, nor do I consider myself an expert. However, for those individuals looking to continue challenging themselves on all levels and are searching for what may be new and exciting word and ideas, I have included a miniature glossary at the back of the book. Said glossary is dedicated to one, Professor Troglodyte.

Namaste.

glossary

A

ar·tic·u·la·tion *(noun)* – the action of putting into words an idea or feeling of a specified type

as·pi·ra·tion *(noun)* – a hope or ambition of achieving something

ar·ray *(noun)* – an impressive display or range of a particular type of thing

a·las *(exclamation)* – an expression of grief, pity, or concern

al·a·bas·ter *(noun or adjective)* – a fine-grained, translucent form of gypsum, typically white, often carved into ornaments

ar·cane *(adjective)* – understood by few; mysterious or secret

am·e·thyst *(noun)* – a precious stone consisting of a violet or purple variety of quartz, a violet or purple color

as·cend *(verb)* – to move upward or climb, to rise

aug·ment *(verb)* – make (something) greater by adding to; increase

a·sun·der *(adverb)* – apart; divided, into pieces

ab·struse *(adjective)* – difficult to understand or obscure

a·mid *(preposition)* – surrounded by; in the middle of, among; in an atmosphere or against a background of

al·lot *(verb)* – to divide or distribute by share or portion; distribute or parcel out; apportion

Atlas *(Greek mythology)* – In Greek mythology, Atlas was a Titan condemned to hold up the sky for eternity

ap·pre·hen·sion *(noun)* – anxiety or fear that something bad or unpleasant will happen, to understand or grasp the concept of

a·kin *(adjective)* – of similar character

B

bask *(verb)* – to lie exposed to warmth and light, typically from the sun, for relaxation and pleasure; to revel in and make the most of something pleasing

be·seech *(verb)* – to ask (someone) urgently and fervently to do something; implore; entreat

bi·sect *(verb)* – to divide into two parts

bril·liant *(adjective or noun)* – bright and radiant; exceptionally clever or talented; a diamond of brilliant cut

C

Caged Bird Sings – *I Know Why the Caged Bird Sings* is a 1969 autobiography about the early years of

American writer and poet Maya Angelou; "With a fearful trill—of things unknown—but longed for still—and his tune is heard—on the distant hill—for the caged bird sings of freedom."

coy *(adjective)* – making a pretense of shyness or modesty that is intended to be alluring, reluctant to give details, especially about something regarded as sensitive; quiet and reserved

cunt *(noun)* – a disparaging term for a person one dislikes or finds extremely disagreeable; a vulgar word that refers to the female genitalia

D

de·sist *(verb)* – cease; abstain, or stop

dis·qui·et *(verb)* – to make (someone) worried or anxious

E

e·nor·mi·ty *(noun)* – on a great or extreme scale, seriousness, or something perceived as bad or morally wrong; a grave crime or sin

en·snare *(verb)* – to influence, capture, or gain control of something or someone

ex·act *(adjective or verb)* – not approximated in any way, precise; demand and obtain (something)

F

for·mal·i·ty *(noun)* – the rigid observance of rules of convention or etiquette, stiffness of behavior or style; a thing that is done simply to comply with requirements of etiquette, regulations, or custom

filch *(verb)* – pilfer or steal in a casual way

H

har·row·ing *(adjective)* – acutely distressing

hum·bly *(adjective)* – behaving in a manner marked by meekness; modesty in behavior, attitude, or spirit; not arrogant or prideful.; showing deferential or submissive respect

I

in·nate *(adjective)* – inborn, natural; originating in the mind

im·part *(verb)* – to make (information) known; communicate, bestow

id·i·om *(noun)* – a phrase or a fixed expression that has a figurative, or sometimes literal, meaning

ir·ref·u·ta·ble *(adjective)* – impossible to deny or disprove

in·sa·tia·ble *(adjective)* – (of an appetite or desire) impossible to satisfy; (of a person) having an insatiable appetite or desire for something

in·quire *(verb)* – ask for information from someone; investigate; look into

J

jad·ed *(adjective)* – made dull, apathetic, or cynical by experience or by disappointment; the end result of having a steady flow of negative experiences, disappointments, and unfulfillment fed into a person until they come to a point of emotional arrest and succumb to disillusionment; an individual who has experienced more energy than he or she is spiritually allotted and is left feeling empty, disheartened, disenchanted

L

la·tent *(adjective)* – (of a quality or state) existing but not yet developed or manifest; hidden; concealed; (of a bud, resting stage, etc.) lying dormant or hidden until circumstances are suitable for

lin·ger·ing *(adjective)* – lasting for a longer time or slow to end

leer *(verb)* – look or gaze in an unpleasant, malicious, or lascivious way

le·ga·to *(adverb)* – in a smooth, flowing manner, without breaks between notes

M

man·i·fest *(adjective)* – to display or show (a quality or feeling) by one's acts or appearance; demonstrate

mi·rage *(noun)* – an optical illusion; something that appears real or possible but is not in fact so

Midas *(noun)* – (classical Greek mythology), Midas was a king who was granted one wish by the god Dionysus. Greedy for riches, Midas wished that everything he touched would turn to gold.

mag·ni·tude *(noun)* – the great size, extent, or importance of something; a number that shows the brightness of a star, or a number that shows the power of an earthquake

mag·nif·i·cent *(adjective)* – impressively beautiful, elaborate, or extravagant; striking

me·an·der *(noun)* – a winding or intricate course suggestive of aimless or listless wandering

N

nom de plume *(noun)* – a pen name *(nom de plume, or literary double)* is a pseudonym (or, in some cases an otherwise unused variant of their real name) adopted by an author and printed on the title page or by-line of their works in place of their "real" name

no·tion *(noun)* – a conception of or belief about something; an impulse or desire, especially one of a whimsical kind

O

ob·scure *(adjective or verb)* – not discovered or known about; uncertain; kept from being seen; conceal

P

po·et·ry *(noun)* – literary work in which special attention and intensity is given to distinctive style and rhythm; a characterized quality of beauty and intensity of emotion; the art of rhythmical composition, written or spoken, for exciting pleasure by beautiful, imaginative, or elevated thoughts

pleas·ant·ry *(noun)* – an inconsequential remark made as part of a polite conversation, a mild joke

pro·found *(adjective)* – penetrating or entering deeply into subjects of thought or knowledge; having deep insight or understanding: originating in or penetrating to the depths of one's being; (of a state, quality, or emotion) very great or intense; (of a person or statement) having or showing great knowledge; the vast depth of the ocean or of the mind

Q

qui·es·cent *(adjective)* – in a state or period of inactivity or dormancy, being at rest; quiet; still; or motionless

R

Rose That Grew From Concrete *(noun)* – *The Rose That Grew from Concrete* is a posthumous album based on the poetry/writings of Tupac Amaru Shakur, released in 2000

re·flec·tion *(noun)* – a thought, idea, or option formed or remarked as a result of meditation; an often obscure or indirect inquiry of the mind; consideration of some subject matter, hypothesis, or purpose

rev·er·ie *(noun)* – a state of dreamy meditation or fanciful musing, a state of being pleasantly lost in one's thoughts; a daydream, an instrumental piece suggesting a dreamy or musing state, a fanciful or impractical idea or theory

re·coil *(verb)* – the backward momentum caused by discharged energy or to suddenly retreat or flinch back in fear, disapproval or exhaustion; to move away from

S

sol·ace *(noun)* – comfort or consolation in a time of distress or sadness

sti·fel *(verb)* – to make (someone) unable to breathe properly; suffocate, choke, asphyxiate, smother, gag; restrain (a reaction) or stop oneself from acting on (an emotion)

si·de·re·al *(adjective)* – of or with respect to the distant stars (i.e., the constellations)

se·ren·i·ty *(noun)* – the state of being calm, peaceful, and untroubled; the state or quality of being serene, calm, or tranquil

sul·ly *(verb)* – to damage the purity or integrity of, or defile; to soil, stain, or tarnish; to mar the purity or luster of

smit·ten *(verb)* – to be strongly attracted to someone or something; overwhelmed or struck by something, usually love

sub·mis·sive *(adjective)* – inclined or ready to submit or yield to the authority of another; unresistingly or humbly obedient; to conform to the authority or will of another; meekly obedient or passive

sul·try *(adjective)* – (of the atmosphere or mood) hot and humid., attractive in a way that suggests a passionate nature, or causes feelings of erotic desire

sul·len *(adjective)* – a gloomy or sulky disposition; a mood or nature characterized by silence or reserve

scrab·ble *(verb)* – to scratch or grope around with one's fingers to find, collect, or hold onto something; to franticly reach for

T

trep·i·da·tion *(noun)* – a feeling of fear or agitation about something that may happen

trans·fig·ure *(verb)* – transform into something more beautiful or elevated

tempt·ress *(noun)* – a woman who tempts someone to do something, typically an attractive woman who sets out to allure or seduce someone

third eye *(noun)* – The third eye (also known as the inner eye) is a mystical and esoteric concept referring to a speculative invisible eye which provides perception beyond ordinary sight. In certain dharmic spiritual traditions such as Hinduism, the third eye refers to the ajna, or brow, chakra

trog·lo·dyte *(noun)* – (especially in prehistoric times) a person who lived in a cave, a hermit; a person who is regarded as being deliberately ignorant or old-fashioned

U

un·earth *(verb)* – to find in the ground by digging; to discover (something hidden, lost, or kept secret) by investigation or searching

un·yield·ing *(adjective)* – (of a mass or structure) not giving way to pressure; hard or solid; (of a person or their behavior) unlikely to be swayed; resolute

Utopia *(noun)* – The term utopia was coined by the Greek Philosopher Sir Thomas More in his 1516 book *Utopia,* describing a fictional island society in the Atlantic Ocean. The word comes from the Greek: *οὐ* ("not") and *τόπος* ("place") and means "no-place," and strictly describes any non-existent society 'described in considerable detail

u·biq·ui·tous *(adjective)* – present, appearing, or found everywhere

un·bear·a·ble *(adjective)* – not able to be endured or tolerated

un·be·com·ing *(adjective)* – not flattering; (of a person's attitude or behavior) not fitting or appropriate; unseemly

un·re·al *(adjective)* – so strange as to appear imaginary; not seeming real; unrealistic

un·sound *(adjective)* – not safe or robust; in poor condition; not based on sound evidence or reasoning and therefore unreliable; (of a person) not competent, reliable, or holding acceptable views

V

vague·ly *(adverb)* – in a way that is uncertain, indefinite, or unclear; roughly; slightly

vig·or *(noun)* – physical strength and good health; legal or binding force; validity

vi·sion *(noun)* – the faculty or state of being able to see; an experience of seeing someone or something in a dream or trance, or as a supernatural apparition; imagine

vent *(noun or verb)* – an opening that allows air, gas, or liquid to pass out of or into a confined space; the expression or release of a strong emotion, energy, etc.; to give free expression to (a strong emotion)

W

wit·ty *(adjective)* – showing or characterized by quick and inventive verbal humor

I am an Artist, an Activist, and a Healer; who enjoys expressing herself via an array of mediums. I am kindly but reserved, pleasant yet stern. I am rationally irrational, imaginative, and determined; But the word I feel best defines me, is Passionate. Ophelia Marcus is my unofficial *nom de plume.* The name is a representation of both the feminine and masculine energies within me. Energy that contrasts that which is light from dark. In this obscure state, I have learned to love my shadow and find comfort in the stillness. I am the result of my deepest consciousness breaching the surface. This publication is a collection of my artistically interpreted thoughts and experiences I had during my spiritual awakening. It is meant to kindle mindfulness and bring about a sense of peace to those going through troubled times.

Namaste.

Apryl Yvonne Scott

Spiritual Advisor

PHONE   (857) 256-1607

EMAIL   WrestlessCommunications@gmail.com

YOUTUBE   Wrestless Communications

INSTAGRAM   @wrestlesscommunications

FACEBOOK   @Apryl Yvonne Scott

www.ingramcontent.com/pod-product-compliance
Lightning Source LLC
Chambersburg PA
CBHW032049040426
42449CB00007B/1046